YOUR LIFE'S PURPOSE

UNCOVER WHAT REALLY FULFILLS YOU

MICHAEL J. LOSIER

bestselling author of *Law of Attraction*

RosettaBooks®

New York 2017

For information, please contact RosettaBooks at production@rosettabooks.com, or by mail at One Exchange Plaza, Suite 2002, 55 Broadway, New York, NY 10006.

RosettaBooks editions are available to the trade through Ingram distribution services, ipage.ingramcontent.com or (844) 749-4857. For special orders, catalogues, events, or other information, please write to production@rosettabooks.com.

First edition published 2017 by RosettaBooks

Cover design by Lauren Harms
Interior design by Brehanna Ramirez
Interior illustrations by Matt Brossard and Brehanna Ramirez
Author photo by Conrad Jay

Library of Congress Control Number: 2016958556
ISBN-13 (print): 978-0-7953-5035-1
ISBN-13 (epub): 978-0-7953-5036-8

www.RosettaBooks.com

Printed in the United States of America

CONTENTS

INTRODUCTION

MY TWO EARLIER BOOKS, *Law of Attraction* and *Law of Connection*, were about helping people bring more of what they want and less of what they don't want into every aspect of their life, including their professional and personal relationships. Over time, however, through talking to people individually as well as in seminars and teleclasses, I came to understand that many people were not consciously aware of *what* they want and need in order to make their lives more joyful and fulfilling.

This was troubling because it was clear to me that if they didn't know what was lacking, they wouldn't know where to focus their energies in order to fill the void they were feeling.

Then, in 2010, when I was in Malaysia teaching people about the Law of Attraction, a man named Siva who was one of my hosts asked me to tell him more about how he could discover his Fulfillment Needs. He had heard me talk about the fact that all the things related to my work—leading seminars, doing book signings, TV, radio, and keynote speaking—were things that fulfilled me. He knew I made decisions quickly and had often heard me say, "That would *not* fulfill me," or "That *would* fulfill me," so he wanted to know how he could do that for himself.

Within one hour of asking the right questions, and using some history and intuitive ideas, I walked Siva through the formula I'm now providing in this book. In just that short time, he was able to uncover his Top 4 Fulfillment Needs and understand what would and would not provide them.

By that time it had become clear to me that I needed to take a step back and teach the people who were participating in my seminars and teleclasses, as well as my readers, how to discover their own Fulfillment Needs so that they could use the information in *Law of Attraction* and *Law of Connection* more effectively.

Discovering your Fulfillment Needs is a process; it's not some magical gift I've been given. In fact, I wasn't always conscious of my own needs as I am now; I took myself through the steps I'll be taking with you to arrive at the clarity I now enjoy.

We all must do some things that don't fulfill us some of the time, but the goal should be to choose things that *do* fulfill us as often as possible. To many people, that sounds selfish. However, taking care of your Fulfillment Needs isn't only about taking care of yourself; it's also about determining and honoring the needs of others. By doing that you will enrich your personal and professional relationships and, therefore, bring more joy into your own life.

This book is going to take you through the processes that will lead you to discover your Top 4 Fulfillment Needs, and show you how to bring more of what you need into your life. Are you in? Then turn the page.

—Michael

AIMS OF THIS BOOK

1. To assist you in uncovering and identifying what fulfills you.

2. To teach you how to integrate your Fulfillment Needs in all areas of your life.

3. To encourage you to consider your Fulfillment Needs when making decisions about your career, your relationships, and your personal choices.

FORMULA FOR LIVING A FULFILLING LIFE

UNDERSTANDING

- Your Life's Purpose
- What Fulfillment Needs Are
- The Fulfillment Needs List
- How to Interpret Your Fulfillment Needs

UNCOVERING

- Your Career Fulfillment Needs
- Your Relationship Fulfillment Needs
- Your Self Fulfillment Needs

APPLYING

- Now That I Know, What Do I Do?
- In Your Relationships
- Using the Law of Attraction

THIS BOOK IS A
SERIES OF PROCESSES

THIS IS A SELF-HELP book, meaning that you will learn how to go through these processes yourself. Follow the steps, do the work, and finish each process before moving on to the next.

Your reward will be a clear understanding of what fulfills you—your Top 4 Fulfillment Needs.

YOUR IDEAL OUTCOME AFTER COMPLETING THE PROCESSES

AS YOU'LL SOON LEARN, you have needs that, when met, allow you to feel fulfilled in your life.

Some needs may seem less important than others. They are not your strongest or most important needs.

Some needs, however, will emerge as very strong and very important, and you will find yourself getting excited about getting them fulfilled. These will be your Top 4 Fulfillment Needs.

Ideally, once you've completed the processes in this book, you'll have uncovered your Top 4 Fulfillment Needs and learned how to use them to help make decisions in your work, relationships, and all areas of your life.

Your reward
for doing the work
will be a better
understanding of what
fulfills you so you can
make the decisions
that bring you joy.

WHAT OTHERS ARE
SAYING NOW THAT THEY KNOW
THEIR TOP 4

"BEFORE I START SOMETHING, I check to see if it matches my Top 4 Fulfillment Needs and if I'm vibrating positively toward it. I can tell by my excitement level." —Rita

"I have been using this knowledge in many ways: 1) In relationships, I have been confident to ask for the fulfillment of these needs from my family (a new request). 2) When I am asked to do a project, I am aware of my needs, and if it is not going to be a match, I decline. 3) In looking for a new job, I am clear about my search and what will give me joy."
—Anne Maree

"I feel more confident in pursuing my roles and relationships with people. My ambitions are better understood/categorized by me. I understand why I have made choices in life that were not necessarily good but were really born out of a need that felt familiar to one of the Top 4 listed. It helps me now to redirect my energy to the things and people that will serve my purpose and me. It helps me understand and zero in on key ideas of my purpose/passions." —Elizabeth

"I turn away everything in my life that does not give me a fulfillment need. I have completely changed since I have identified my Fulfillment Needs. I've read a lot of [Michael's] material, and I took action on several major areas of my life, including my love life. It's like a miracle; I am getting more and more of what I want, and after a truly terrible four years, I feel peaceful and contented. It's amazing!" —Sheena

"When I am deciding what I want to do, it helps to know what will be the most fulfilling for me. It was easy to figure out the need most important to me, but I had some difficulty with the last two." —Gwynne

"The biggest surprise to me was my need for security, and the other was to admit how much I want to be appreciated and get acknowledgment and recognition for making a difference. I've been looking for opportunities that will deliver security (which is totally new for me). This means that I've been looking for opportunities that can lead to others and am designing delivery packages that will continue over time and are not a one-off. I've become much *more filled with intention about how to capitalize on all my know-how and looking at my future in terms of taking care of myself."* —Maureen

"I understand why I have been doing what I'm doing, and it makes more sense now. I have and will be deliberate in putting my Top 4 Fulfillment Needs into all my action plans, whether it be at work or personal activities." —Martin

"Whenever I engage in something or I'm in the process of making a choice about something, I ask myself if my Fulfillment Needs are being met. I use this in my work life all the time, and I've found that I keep attracting interesting and fulfilling projects! It's all very rewarding. I'm much happier and more fulfilled in my work life than I've ever been! I also keep my needs top of mind with relationships... very important to feeling a sense of connection that's good and full of joy!" —Rhonda

UNDERSTANDING

WHAT EXACTLY ARE
FULFILLMENT NEEDS?

I COINED THE TERM "Fulfillment Needs" after hearing many people talk about being unfulfilled. To me, this meant that they were missing some of the things that brought them fulfillment—some of their needs were not being met.

You may be familiar with other terms used to describe this category of needs, such as:

- Personal Core Values
- Motivators
- Life Purpose
- Calling
- Soul's Purpose
- Meaning of Life

- Driving Needs
- Vocation
- Reason for Being
- Personal Calling

What I want you to understand is that certain needs, when we get them met, bring us joy. These needs fulfill us, hence the term "Fulfillment Needs."

I like to make complex processes easy to understand and apply. Those of you who have read my other books, *Law of Attraction* and *Law of Connection*, will recognize that my writing style is the same in this book.

Certain needs, when met, fulfill us, hence the term "Fulfillment Needs."

HOW FULFILLMENT NEEDS ARE CONNECTED TO THE PURPOSE OF YOUR LIFE

WHAT IS THE PURPOSE
OF YOUR LIFE?

PERHAPS YOU OR SOMEONE you know is struggling to discover their life's purpose—what they are on the planet to do. Sound familiar?

It's a *big* question: "What is the purpose of my life?"

Observe these two conversations on the subject of life's purpose. Notice that the end results of the two conversations are similar.

Conversation with a teacher:

> MICHAEL: What would you say is the purpose of your life?
>
> TEACHER: The purpose in my life is to teach and educate others.
>
> MICHAEL: When you are teaching and educating others, how does that make you feel?
>
> TEACHER: When teaching, I experience great contentment, satisfaction, and joy.

MICHAEL: So teaching brings you joy?

TEACHER: Yes, teaching brings me joy.

MICHAEL: If you were in a job or a relationship where you were unable to teach and educate someone, how would that make you feel?

TEACHER: If I could not teach and educate others, I would not feel helpful or inspired; I would not feel any joy.

Conversation with an artist:

MICHAEL: What would you say is the purpose of your life?

ARTIST: Definitely my artwork and creativity.

MICHAEL: How do you feel when you are working on art projects and can be creative?

ARTIST: It's very uplifting for me.

MICHAEL: Being creative and working on art projects brings you joy?

ARTIST: Yes, a lot.

MICHAEL: If you had a job where you were unable to be creative or do your artwork, how would that make you feel?

ARTIST: If I had a job that did not allow me to be creative or create art, I would not feel any joy.

Ask a hundred people to define the purpose of their life, and you'll get a hundred answers. The answers will cover a range of areas. Then expand your questioning by asking, "To achieve what?" And finally ask, "And what do you get out of it?"

HOW FULFILLMENT NEEDS ARE CONNECTED TO THE PURPOSE OF YOUR LIFE

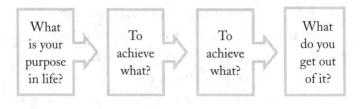

What is your purpose in life?	To achieve what?	To achieve what?	What do you get out of it?
To sing	To please audiences	So they will love and admire me	Joy
To dance	To release energy and be fit	Happiness	Joy
To race cars	To get a thrill	I can ignore my boring life	Joy

To be a physician	To help people through illness	I feel useful	Joy
To teach	To help others reach their potential	So they can be fulfilled	Joy
To heal the planet	To allow us to live here for a long time	I'll feel better about what I do	Joy
To be a caregiver for elders	To provide care for others	So their lives can be more comfortable	Joy
To be on stage	To share my talents with others	To please them	Joy
To be a high school baseball coach	To help kids achieve their potential	I feel fulfilled	Joy

WHAT DO YOU FEEL WHEN LIVING YOUR LIFE'S PURPOSE?

JOY. SIMPLE ENOUGH—JOY. **You may say bliss, high vibes, ecstasy, fantastic, wonderful, or similar expressions. They all mean the same thing: JOY.**

You know how well life works out when you are experiencing happiness and joy. On the other hand, you also know what life can be like when you are *not* experiencing joy.

As shown in this diagram, there is a direct relationship between how you feel and the results you're getting—that is, how well your life is working out.

GOT JOY?	VIBES GENERATED	RESULTS
Anna experiences joy in her relation-ships	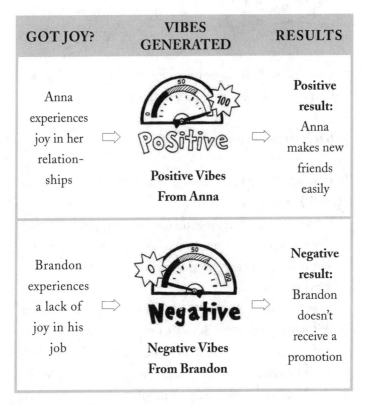 **Positive Vibes From Anna**	**Positive result:** Anna makes new friends easily
Brandon experiences a lack of joy in his job	**Negative Vibes From Brandon**	**Negative result:** Brandon doesn't receive a promotion

So, Joy Is the Target?

If joy is the target, the question you need to ask yourself is, "What brings me joy?"

Many people are unsure, confused, and don't know how to answer that question. Some people don't even believe it's possible or okay to feel joy.

What brings you joy?

Is it a list of physical things? Relationships? A job or career? Family?

These are the strategies you use to bring you joy. Once you've answered that question, you need to ask yourself, "What is it about that physical thing, relationship, or job that brings me joy?"

That second question is designed to tell you what Fulfillment Needs are getting met through your strategies for achieving joy. It is the big question this book will help you answer. You will learn what Fulfillment Needs are and, more importantly, you will uncover your own Top 4.

REACHING THE TARGET
THROUGH FULFILLMENT

WHEN YOU IDENTIFY YOUR *Fulfillment Needs*, you are able to create and attract the *strategies* to get these needs met. When you get your needs met, you experience *JOY*.

There is a direct
relationship between
how you feel and the
results you're getting.

YOUR LEVEL OF FULFILLMENT IS EQUAL TO YOUR LEVEL OF JOY

YOUR FEELINGS ARE CONSTANTLY reflecting and measuring the joy that you feel in every situation. While we sometimes have to do things that don't bring us joy, the goal is to choose things that *do* bring joy as often as possible.

Pay attention to your feelings as you try different strategies that may bring you joy. It's important that you become "selfish" about the level at which you choose to be fulfilled.

To experience joy as often as you'd like sometimes means making choices that seem selfish, but what you're really demonstrating is self-care. Care enough about yourself to make yourself happy!

Selfish =
Self-Care

GUILT AND DISCOMFORT?

YES, SOME PEOPLE RESIST or feel guilty about making choices that make *them* feel good.

If you are feeling guilty or resistant, consider that when you are feeling good about yourself, you can help serve others better. We all want to be around people who uplift us, and those people are the ones who are positive, because they are experiencing joy in their lives.

You were attracted to this book for a reason.

- Isn't it time *you* felt fulfilled in your life?
- How would your life be different if you were making choices that made you feel good?
- How would your life be different if *you* were that friend or parent about whom people say, "He/she is the most uplifting person in my life"?

You probably care about what you eat, what music you listen to, and what you wear. Now you need to get better at practicing that same kind of self-care when it comes to choosing a job, a romantic partner, or friendships.

You need to pay attention to when you're being fulfilled and when you're not—in relationships, at home, with neighbors, with your hobbies, and in your career. It's all about Fulfillment.

KNOWING YOUR TOP 4 WILL HELP
YOU MAKE BETTER DECISIONS

WHEN YOU KNOW WHAT your Top 4 Fulfillment Needs are, you'll be able to use that information to help you make decisions. When it comes time to choose a new career or a new relationship, your feelings will measure the level of joy you feel when making your decision. That will indicate whether or not you're making the right choice for yourself. You can pay attention to your feelings when making all kinds of decisions—from buying a new home to deciding where to go on your next vacation. The opportunities are abundant.

Couples should also pay special attention to each other's feelings to be sure that both their needs are getting met when making important decisions.

KNOWING OTHERS' TOP 4 CAN IMPROVE RELATIONSHIPS— AT HOME AND AT WORK

WHEN YOU KNOW AND support other people's Fulfillment Needs, you can discuss and improve the harmony and communication in your relationships.

In a later section, I'll discuss ways that couples can create strategies for discovering, understanding, and satisfying each other's Fulfillment Needs.

I'll also discuss how you can apply those same strategies to your work environment to support your employees, coworkers, and managers in meeting their needs, which will result in everyone feeling more fulfilled.

Once you identify your own Top 4 and experience the fulfillment from getting them met on a regular basis, you'll want to share these processes with others and work together to support each other in meeting your respective Fulfillment Needs.

THIS SECTION SUMMARY AND CHECKLIST

*How Fulfillment Needs Are Connected
to the Purpose of Your Life*

IN THIS SECTION WE discovered:

☐ The purpose of life is JOY.

☐ Joy is the target.

☐ What Fulfillment Needs are.

☐ There are strategies we can use to get our
Fulfillment Needs met.

☐ Our feelings measure our level of joy.

☐ Knowing our Fulfillment Needs will help us
make better decisions.

☐ Knowing and supporting others' Fulfillment
Needs can improve our relationships.

THE THIRTY MOST COMMON FULFILLMENT NEEDS AND WHAT THEY MEAN

MASTER FULFILLMENT
NEEDS LIST

ON THE NEXT PAGE, I'VE listed in alphabetical order the thirty most common Fulfillment Needs. In the many years I've been helping people uncover their Fulfillment Needs, these are the thirty that people most often identify as important.

At this point, I'm just introducing you to the list of Fulfillment Needs. Throughout the book you'll be working with this list to determine which ones are most important to you. For now, just read through the list and notice the words that resonate with you.

MASTER FULFILLMENT
NEEDS LIST

Accomplishment	Freedom
Achievement	Fun
Acknowledgment	Importance
Adventure	Inclusion
Appreciation	Individuality
Approval	Influence
Attention	Integrity
Autonomy	Intimacy
Challenge	Leadership
Community	Power
Connection	Recognition
Contribution	Safety
Control	Security
Creativity	Specialness
Fairness	Uniqueness

INTERPRETIVE GLOSSARY

SOME PEOPLE ARE UNCERTAIN about the meanings of some of the Fulfillment Needs on the list. Therefore, I've compiled a glossary of Fulfillment Needs to help you clarify the meanings of the words.

I've called this an "interpretive glossary" because the definitions reflect the most common interpretations I've gathered from a variety of people who have worked through these processes.

Some of the words may not mean the same thing to you as they do to other people. That's okay. Later in this section, I'll explain how you can reframe the meanings to fit your own interpretation of the words. For our purposes, there are no right or wrong definitions. It's *your* interpretation that matters!

See the Interpretive Glossary of Fulfillment Needs at the end of this book.

CAN I ADD NEW FULFILLMENT
WORDS TO THE LIST?

WHEN SOME PEOPLE FIRST see the list, they feel there's a Fulfillment Need missing and want to add a word. Some words that may seem like Fulfillment Needs to you often have layers of meaning that can be peeled back like the layers of an onion to uncover a Fulfillment Need that is on the list.

Uncovering the Real Fulfillment Need

When someone wants to add a new need to the list, I use two questions to help them determine if there's another Fulfillment Need at the core. Those questions are: "For what purpose?" and "What will *that* provide?"

Two of the most common needs people ask about adding are "money" and "intellectual stimulation." On the next page you will find examples of clients' responses to those questions. Notice that, in each of these examples, after answering "What will *that* provide?" a layer is peeled back and another Fulfillment Need is uncovered.

Is there a word you'd like to add to the list? If so, it's a good idea to test it to see if it's truly a Fulfillment Need.

Here's what some of my clients discovered when they tested "money" and "intellectual stimulation" with the two questions.

I NEED MONEY:

Question 1: For what purpose?	Question 2: What will *that* provide?
a) So I can take time off and travel more.	**a)** A sense of *freedom*.
b) So I can donate money to people who need it.	**b)** The feeling of making a differ-ence—a *contribution*.
c) So I can better provide for my family.	**c)** A feeling of *safety* and *security*.

Notice that it's what money *provides* that uncovers the real Fulfillment Need.

Now let's look at "intellectual stimulation."

I NEED <u>INTELLECTUAL STIMULATION</u>:	
Question 1: For what purpose?	**Question 2:** What will *that* provide?
a) So I won't be bored. ⟹	**a)** A mental *challenge*.
b) So I can exchange ideas with someone I "click" with. ⟹	**b)** A feeling of *connection*.
c) So I can increase my learning and knowledge. ⟹	**c)** A feeling of *accomplishment* and *importance*.

Now it's your turn. How would you fill out this chart? (Blank worksheets are available under the Worksheet Tab at YourLifesPurposeBook.com.)

I NEED _ _ _ _ _ _ _ _ _ _

I NEED _ _ _ _ _ _ _ _ _ _

Question 1:	Question 2:
For what purpose?	What will *that* provide?

So... ⇨

So... ⇨

So... ⇨

IT'S YOUR OWN DEFINITION AND PERCEPTION THAT COUNT

AS YOU MOVE THROUGH the processes to uncover your Top 4 Fulfillment Needs, it's important to remember that *your interpretation and perception of the words are what really count,* even if they differ from other people's interpretations.

You may sense that a need is important to you but feel uncomfortable with your or other people's negative interpretation of it. If so, you can shift your interpretation to one that makes you more comfortable. Notice here that three different people have three different interpretations of the Fulfillment Need Control.

What is your interpretation of the word "control"?

_____

_____

_____

_____

_____

_____

_____

_____

_____

_____

_____

_____

_____

_____

FEELING GOOD ABOUT YOUR FULFILLMENT NEEDS

IN ADDITION TO FEELING uncomfortable with the meaning of the needs you identify as important, you may perhaps feel that you don't deserve to get these needs met. Or you may feel some apprehension about the changes you imagine you'll have to make in order to get your needs met.

When I uncovered my top Fulfillment Needs, I too felt some discomfort.

My Top 4 Fulfillment Needs are:

- Attention

- Influence

- Intimacy

- Freedom

I realized it was important to reframe the meanings of these words into something that felt more comfortable to me.

How you *feel* about the word is most important. You can make a Fulfillment Need word feel just right for you by creating your own meaning for the word. Let me share my personal process of reframing my Fulfillment Needs.

REFRAMING THE MEANING

My Process of Interpretation

I'VE ALWAYS KNOWN THAT I liked attention, but I'd hear others' voices in my mind judging attention as something negative—it was "showing off." Given what I'd heard others say about it, I felt uncomfortable and embarrassed about the fact that Attention was my top Fulfillment Need. I knew I had to reframe the word in order to be comfortable with it. Reframing means to see or hear the word from a different point of view, or to give it a different meaning.

Here are my Top 4 Fulfillment Needs and a brief description of how I changed their meanings to fit or make sense to me.

I reframed the word "attention" into **Attentiveness**.

I really like it when students are attentive and honor my time with them. This includes listening and, of course, being influenced by me in a positive way.

I reframed the word "influence" into **Positive Influence**.

I like it when people tell me what a positive influence my books or seminars had on them, or when they quote something specific from my book that changed their way of thinking. I like influencing people in a positive way.

MICHAEL J. LOSIER

I reframed the word "intimacy" into Into-Me-See.

(When you let someone into your personal life, you create intimacy.)

"Intimacy" is one of those words that always needs to be interpreted. For me, it is about conversation. For example, a coffee meeting with me would include conversation of a personal nature—such as discussing how the Law of Attraction is working in your life, or talking about success, personal growth, or relationships. All these topics are a form of intimacy to me.

I was comfortable with the word **Freedom.**

My fourth Fulfillment Need is Freedom. For me, freedom means the ability to decide how I spend my time. Time is one of my values. I cherish my time with good friends. I honor my time and other people's time. So when I build my speaking and training business, I always consider how much time I will be away from home.

It's *Your* Interpretation That Matters

THIS SECTION SUMMARY AND CHECKLIST

The Top Thirty Fulfillment Needs and What They Mean

IN THIS SECTION WE discovered:

- ☐ There are thirty most common Fulfillment Needs from which to choose

- ☐ We can test other words to see if they are true Fulfillment Needs

- ☐ We can refer to the glossary of Fulfillment Needs to clarify the meaning of some words

- ☐ We can reframe the meanings to work for us

- ☐ It's *our own* interpretation of the words that matters most

UNCOVERING

THREE COMMON AREAS
OF FULFILLMENT

ALTHOUGH OUR GOAL IS to be fulfilled in all areas of our lives, this section will focus on three of the most common areas people choose to work on:

1. Career Fulfillment
2. Relationship Fulfillment
3. Self Fulfillment

For each of these areas you will be introduced to a student using the Uncovering Processes in this book:

Career Fulfillment:
You will meet Trevor, a successful accountant who has worked many years and is feeling less fulfilled at work.

Relationship Fulfillment:
You will meet Lucy, who is tired of the dating scene and wants to figure out what would fulfill her with her ideal partner.

Self Fulfillment:
You will meet Sophie, who is feeling her life could use some change—she is bored, restless, and now understands she is not fulfilled in her life.

CAREER FULFILLMENT

TREVOR'S STORY

 HI, MY NAME IS Trevor, and I'm a tax accountant—a very successful one, mind you. It's an important job and I take it seriously. There's a lot riding on the accuracy of my work. I'm a respected professional and have earned the trust of my clients, who rely on me to save them money and bureaucratic headaches.

I've climbed the ladder, paid my dues, and now own a thriving business that employs two people and generates a healthy income for me and my family. Although my family life is quite wonderful—I really love my wife, my kids, my dog, my house—there is still something missing.

There's a nagging thought I have... sometimes a quiet yearning... for something else to make my life more complete. I think some important need or needs are not being met by the life I've built. I'm also keenly aware of time passing and don't want to live with the regret that I didn't take action to make a more fulfilling life.

When I was young, I was taught by my parents that finding my place in life and finding a secure job were key values. Being self-sufficient, reliable, and a good provider were the highest aspirations I could attain. Well, I've attained them, and I still want more. I don't want more stuff or people in my life, I just want a deeper satisfaction. So, what am I missing?

I think back on my grandparents, who passed away years ago and who were from a much earlier generation. They were farmers who took real pride in their land and the contribution they made to their community. They always seemed to be deeply content with their lives and their choices, even though I can't imagine living as simply or with as few resources as them. Clearly, they found happiness without having a big house, a fancy car, expensive vacations, or surplus spending money in their bank accounts, etc. What was their secret?

If I'm to be really honest—and it almost seems sacrilegious to even think this—I have come to the conclusion that I need to give up my current job and find work that I truly love. It's the one area of my life that feels emotionally flat. It's been a long time since I was excited to go to work. In the beginning, building my business was fun because it was creative and I was taking a risk. Now that I'm established, the hours spent reviewing numbers, receipts, and forms hold little stimulation for me. Is this all there is?

I've decided I need help to figure this out. I'm going to use the Fulfillment Needs process to drill down and see what kind of work would really get me firing on all cylinders. I'm excited just thinking that my work could be a source of joy for me—like my family life. So here goes…

THE UNCOVERING PROCESS

THERE ARE FOUR EXERCISES used to help uncover Fulfillment Needs:

> Exercise #1: Narrowing Down the Fulfillment Needs List
>
> Exercise #2: Discovering Worksheet— Current Job
>
> Exercise #3: Discovering Worksheet— Past Job
>
> Exercise #4: Discovering Worksheet— Worst Job

EXERCISE #1: Narrowing Down the List

From what I understand about Fulfillment Needs, if they get met, I feel joy. Simple as that. It's really such an elegant and intuitive approach to living a happy, fulfilled life. But what makes me joyful doesn't necessarily rock someone else's world. I need to use a bit of process and structure to help get clear on *where my joy lies*.

So I'm going to start by reviewing the Master List of Fulfillment Needs and narrowing it down to words that have particular meaning and resonance for me. I like to use my gut feelings and spontaneous reactions as a guide to decision making. I reflected on each word and did a quick measure of my feeling response to each. Without too much deliberation, I crossed off the words that don't really stick. Here's my narrowed-down list and a few notes explaining my sifting process:

Trevor's Narrowed-Down List of Fulfillment Needs	
Accomplishment Achievement	Accomplishment and achievement are sort of similar, but reaching a big goal for me is thrilling!
~~Acknowledgment~~ Adventure	I like the unknown and depending on my own resources. Not sure if this is a successful work quality. :)
~~Appreciation~~ Approval	Don't like to admit it...
~~Attention~~ Autonomy	Definitely!
Challenge	My proudest moment was opening my own business.
~~Community~~ Connection	Yeah, okay.
Contribution	Yup.
Control	Kind of a harsh word, but maybe it fits.
Creativity	Yum!
~~Fairness~~ Freedom	Oh! That one rings a bell!
Fun	Seems kind of a childish word, but I'll keep it.

~~Importance~~	
Inclusion	Now that I reflect on it, that word feels pretty good.
Individuality	Yeah, maybe.
Influence	Ooh, that's an interesting feeling in my stomach.
~~Integrity~~	
Intimacy	More so when I think of my family, so… we'll see.
Leadership	My wife would like it, so I better check that one.
~~Power~~	
~~Recognition~~	
~~Safety~~	
Security	That feels interesting, too. Never thought of that.
~~Specialness~~	
Uniqueness	I want to live a unique life, but is that reasonable?

The following chart is an example of what we will use to track Trevor's Fulfillment Needs as they are uncovered in the next three exercises.

Trevor's Personal Fulfillment Needs List			
Exercise #1	**Exercise #2**	**Exercise #3**	**Exercise #4**
Accomplishment			
Achievement			
Adventure			
Approval			
Autonomy			
Challenge			
Connection			
Contribution			
Control			
Creativity			
Freedom			
Fun			
Inclusion			
Individuality			
Influence			
Intimacy			
Leadership			
Security			
Uniqueness			

EXERCISE #2: Current Job

As I've mentioned, I'm a successful, self-employed tax accountant. I like that it pays well, that people trust and rely on me, and that I get to make a complicated process more simple. I also like that I was able to launch and nurture the business myself. It's a big accomplishment to be your own boss, and I must say I enjoy not having someone looking over my shoulder all the time.

The downside of my work is that a lot of time is spent working in isolation. It can take days to unravel bad bookkeeping practices, and I can get frustrated with how much time and money is wasted by other people's inefficiencies. Sometimes, after a less than satisfying workday, I wonder if my life will always be about untangling other people's messes.

Trevor's "Discovering Worksheet": Current Job

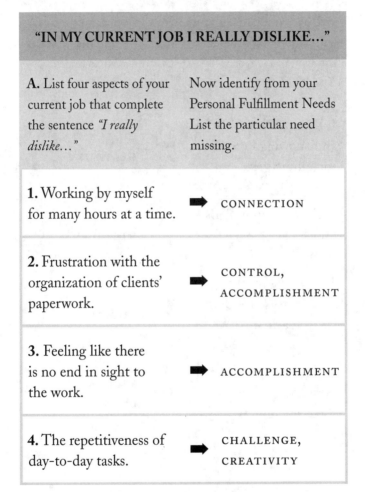

"IN MY CURRENT JOB I REALLY DISLIKE..."

A. List four aspects of your current job that complete the sentence *"I really dislike..."*

Now identify from your Personal Fulfillment Needs List the particular need missing.

1. Working by myself for many hours at a time. ➡ CONNECTION

2. Frustration with the organization of clients' paperwork. ➡ CONTROL, ACCOMPLISHMENT

3. Feeling like there is no end in sight to the work. ➡ ACCOMPLISHMENT

4. The repetitiveness of day-to-day tasks. ➡ CHALLENGE, CREATIVITY

"IN MY CURRENT JOB I LOVE..."

B. List four aspects of your current job that complete the sentence *"I love..."*

Now identify from your Personal Fulfillment Needs List the particular need that is fulfilled.

1. Being self-employed and knowing I created something great. ➡ ACHIEVEMENT, CREATIVITY

2. That it pays well and I don't have money fears. ➡ SECURITY, AUTONOMY

3. Bringing relief to my clients by avoiding tax headaches. ➡ INFLUENCE, INTIMACY

4. The feeling that I can make my own choices about my future. ➡ FREEDOM, AUTONOMY

EXERCISE #3: Past Job

I wasn't always a tax accountant. I had jobs in high school and college and did some other jobs before I decided to commit to my current field. My favorite past job would have to be a six-month gig working as a landscaper before I started college. It paid okay, but the real joy for me was working with my hands in the soil and seeing my efforts grow and bloom (maybe I inherited that from Grandpa). I also loved that I got to be creative with color, texture, shape, and making the new landscaping adapt to the setting. I sometimes drive by the properties I landscaped, and there is an awesome sense of pride and being part of something bigger than myself. When I see a tree towering where I once planted a sapling, or a grapevine I nurtured that is now laden with fruit, I know that something good and lasting came from my work.

To be honest, I didn't love everything about that landscaping job. The hours were long, the pay was mediocre, and my boss was a pain. He never seemed completely satisfied with my work. And there were some days I came home so exhausted from the physical labor that I'd skip dinner and head straight to bed.

Trevor's "Discovering Worksheet": Past Job

"IN MY PAST JOB I REALLY DISLIKED…"	
A. List four aspects of your past job that complete the sentence *"I really disliked…"*	Now identify from your Personal Fulfillment Needs List the particular need that was missing.
1. Working long hours for a mediocre paycheck.	➡ FREEDOM, SECURITY
2. My boss was difficult to work with and was never satisfied.	➡ APPROVAL, INTIMACY
3. The work was often physically exhausting.	➡ FREEDOM, FUN
4. There were no long-term prospects for me.	➡ ACHIEVEMENT

"IN MY PAST JOB I LOVED..."	
B. List four aspects of your past job that complete the sentence *"I loved..."*	Now identify from your Personal Fulfillment Needs List the particular need that was fulfilled.
1. Working with my hands.	➡ CONTRIBUTION
2. Being creative with color and texture.	➡ CREATIVITY, FUN
3. Knowing that my labor had a lasting impact.	➡ INFLUENCE, ACCOMPLISHMENT
4. Working outside.	➡ FREEDOM, AUTONOMY

EXERCISE #4: Worst Job

The worst job I ever had was also before college, when I worked for my older brother at his construction company. It paid crap, my brother was overbearing and bossy, and I had to organize thousands of stupid little "thingies" used to hold concrete forms together. They were a nightmare to untangle, often tossed in a pile after a job was done, covered in chunks of dried concrete. I hated wasting my time cleaning up other people's messes. Couldn't they have been more organized and more respectful of their equipment?

It wasn't all bad, though. I learned patience and that sometimes you just have to keep persevering to get the job done. There was also a camaraderie among the other young guys working there that I miss sometimes in my current job.

Trevor's "Discovering Worksheet": Worst Job

"IN MY WORST JOB I REALLY DISLIKED..."	
A. List four aspects of your worst job that complete the sentence *"I really disliked..."*	Now identify from your Personal Fulfillment Needs List the particular need that was missing.
1. Feeling exploited by getting paid minimum wage.	➡ SECURITY, ACCOMPLISHMENT
2. Wasting my time cleaning up other people's messes.	➡ CONTRIBUTION, INTIMACY
3. Focusing on meaningless and mundane tasks with little to show for it.	➡ FUN, ACCOMPLISHMENT
4. My brother was a terrible, overbearing boss.	➡ FREEDOM

"IN MY WORST JOB I LOVED…"

B. List four aspects of your worst job that complete the sentence *"I loved…"*	Now identify from your Personal Fulfillment Needs List the particular need that was fulfilled.
1. The camaraderie that came from working with others.	➡ CONNECTION
2. Knowing that I was building character.	➡ CHALLENGE
3. Learning about an industry and seeing how a business is run.	➡ CREATIVITY
4. Working outside.	➡ FREEDOM, AUTONOMY

CALCULATING THE RESULTS

NOW TREVOR'S PERSONAL FULFILLMENT Needs chart is filled in. The Fulfillment Need he identified in each exercise is entered on the next page.

Trevor's Personal Fulfillment Needs List			
Exercise #1	**Exercise #2**	**Exercise #3**	**Exercise #4**
➡ Accomplishment	✖ ✖	✖	✖ ✖
Achievement	✖	✖	
Adventure			
Approval		✖	
➡ Autonomy	✖ ✖	✖	✖
Challenge	✖		✖
Connection	✖		✖
Contribution		✖	✖
Control	✖		
➡ Creativity	✖ ✖	✖	✖
➡ Freedom	✖	✖ ✖ ✖	✖ ✖
Fun		✖ ✖	✖
Inclusion			
Individuality			
Influence	✖	✖	
Intimacy	✖	✖	✖
Leadership			
Security	✖	✖	✖
Uniqueness			

TOP 4 FULFILLMENT NEEDS

ACCOMPLISHMENT

AUTONOMY

CREATIVITY

FREEDOM

WHAT CHANGED FOR TREVOR?

IT WAS REALLY ILLUMINATING to go through the exercises. Even just reviewing the full list of Fulfillment Needs made me think, *Wow! Do I have permission to feel this awesome at work? Have I been denying myself all this time?*

When I eventually narrowed the lists of needs down to my Top 4, it all made sense! The process of remembering work experiences that gave me joy and those that I hated really brought clarity. I realize that I need to feel like my work has lasting impact and is life affirming. I want to see the results of my effort and know I've made a difference. I also am clear that whatever direction I go, I have to be in charge—no bosses, no sharing leadership with someone else.

I can now also say that the thing that has been missing in my current occupation and which I now know is a critical need is creativity. The landscaping job allowed me to make something from nothing, to bring life to barren ground, to see the potential waiting to be uncovered.

L

RELATIONSHIP FULFILLMENT

LUCY'S STORY

 MY MOTHER USED TO say, "*Lucy, there are plenty of fish in the sea—just hold your nose and pick one!*" My mom grew up on the East Coast and loved fishing metaphors. She also was very traditional and viewed relationships through the lens of religion and duty. Once you've caught one, you just hold tight and reel him in. Set up a house, have a family, and we'll all live happily ever after. That's what I've been brought up to believe, and that is what shapes the dilemma I face now as I search for a life partner.

As a teenager I imagined falling in love with some handsome, mysterious guy, escaping my hometown in a VW van then driving down to Baja and getting married on the seashore with the light of bioluminescence sparkling around our ankles.

Ever since I finished college, I've been on the lookout for that seashore man, and with each passing year my searching gets all the more urgent.

Consequently, I rush in too fast with men and scare the bejesus out of most of them. More than a few have confessed this to me in "Dear Lucy" letters. I have a collection, you know. It's like I'm playing some crazy version of Beat the Clock. Maybe I'm trying to beat my biological clock.

I do worry I won't find *the one*. I really want children and grandchildren, but I also don't want to settle for the next guy that comes along. I want a life partner who'll be there through thick and thin and who likes babies and picnics and *Star Trek*.

I feel caught between two forces pulling me in different directions. Do I hook one and reel him in, or do I keep searching for the perfect mate? Does my need for security and stability outweigh my need for romance and love?

It wasn't supposed to be like this. Finding my one true love was supposed to happen naturally or miraculously. When did it become so calculated and practical?

I've been inspired to find clarity through a Fulfilment Needs exercise—a way of sorting through what's really important to me and identifying my sources of joy.

THE UNCOVERING PROCESS

THERE ARE FOUR EXERCISES used to help uncover
Fulfillment Needs:

Exercise #1: Narrowing Down the
Fulfillment Needs List

Exercise #2: Discovering Worksheet—
Current Job

Exercise #3: Discovering Worksheet—
Past Job

Exercise #4: Discovering Worksheet—
Worst Job

EXERCISE #1: Narrowing Down the List

Love, love, love! There's my list. That's all I need... Hold on, the word "love" isn't on the Master List of Fulfillment Needs! Maybe that's because love isn't a need. It's more like an action. When I think of needing love, I guess I'm really yearning for the feelings that love makes me feel.

The Master List of Fulfilment Needs is a wide-ranging array of feelings and states of being that we all understand and have experienced. At first glance, I see lots of words that don't fit me at all. I can't even imagine "power" being a fulfillment need for me. This sorting process should be easy.

On the next page is my narrowed-down list of Fulfillment Needs. I surprised myself with some of my choices.

Lucy's Narrowed-Down List of Fulfillment Needs

~~Accomplishment~~

Achievement · Maybe it's my upbringing, but starting a family is a big deal, and I'll be proud to be called Mom.

~~Acknowledgment~~

Adventure · Okay, as long as there's air-conditioning.

~~Appreciation~~

Approval · My mom's opinion matters to me.

Attention

~~Autonomy~~

~~Challenge~~

Community · I feel secure when I know lots of people care about me.

Connection · Similar to community in my mind.

~~Contribution~~

Control · Does that make me controlling?

~~Creativity~~

~~Fairness~~

~~Freedom~~

Fun · I love fun. I like how the word sounds, too.

Importance	I want to be important to other people.
~~Inclusion~~	
Individuality	Yes, but I'm not sure how that reconciles with my dreams.
~~Influence~~	
Integrity	I want that in my partner. Trust is important.
Intimacy	I like being vulnerable.
Leadership	That comes with raising a family.
Power	Now that I'm into this exercise, I can interpret "power" more positively.
Recognition	I guess so.
Safety	I don't want to grow old alone.
Security	Same as above.
Specialness	I am a princess after all.
~~Uniqueness~~	

EXERCISE #2: Current Relationship

Well, I date… a lot… but my current relationship would be Steven. Steven is funny. We laugh all the time. So he certainly meets my fun quotient. A sense of humor makes everything easier. He also wants to travel the world one day, which is one of my dreams, too.

Steven is a bartender at a local dance club. He's out late a lot and constantly surrounded by tipsy, flirty women. He knows it drives me crazy, but that's the job. Couldn't he serve drinks at the veterans' club? It makes me feel so insecure sometimes.

And although there's nothing wrong with bartending, could we buy a house on his wage and could he coparent if he's working until the wee hours? It's too early for me to really go deep with him on this topic, but he seems to lack the ambition to be more than he is.

Fortunately, Steven thinks I'm amazing. When we're together he dotes on me and makes me feel important. He gives me little gifts and massages my feet.

I really like Steven, but ticktock goes my clock, and I can't stop thinking that my dream of a family doesn't include him—at least not with the career he has now.

Lucy's "Discovering Worksheet": Current Relationship

"IN MY CURRENT RELATIONSHIP I REALLY DISLIKE..."	
A. List four aspects of your current relationship that complete the sentence *"I really dislike..."*	Now identify from your Personal Fulfillment Needs List the particular need that is missing.
1. Worrying about fidelity.	➡ SECURITY
2. Feeling he won't be a good provider.	➡ SECURITY
3. Thinking I would have to raise children without support.	➡ SECURITY, CONNECTION
4. His lack of ambition to create a better life.	➡ IMPORTANCE, INTEGRITY

"IN MY CURRENT RELATIONSHIP I LOVE..."

B. List four aspects of your current relationship that complete the sentence *"I love..."*	Now identify from your Personal Fulfillment Needs List the particular need that is fulfilled.
1. My partner's sense of humor.	➡ FUN
2. Sharing the dream of travel.	➡ ADVENTURE
3. Being loved and cherished.	➡ ATTENTION, INTIMACY
4. Feeling like I'm important.	➡ IMPORTANCE

EXERCISE #3: Past Relationship

When I think back on all my past relationships, there is one that really stands out, because at the time it seemed to offer all the promise and security that I had wished for.

Meeting Paul for the first time was electric. He was a university professor who taught quantum mechanics to undergrads. He had such a mesmerizing way of describing how the subatomic world works. I didn't really understand most of what he said, but his enthusiasm was infectious. When he would get lost in one of his deliriously complicated explanations, it almost felt like he was pulling back a curtain and peering into the secrets of the universe.

Paul also had a romantic heart and imagined that one day he'd start a family and settle down. His job paid well and he had tenure, which is about as secure as you can get.

What I didn't love about Paul was his aversion to emotional intimacy. When I pushed, he pulled away. When I cried, he patted my back and made comforting sounds, but he never wanted to really understand me. Being around Paul meant I had to put my own personality aside and let him fill the space.

Maybe because he was brilliant and adored by his students he didn't really understand vulnerability and humility.

I got tired of pursuing a heart that just wouldn't open. It made me feel bad about myself—like I was unimportant and unlovable.

Lucy's "Discovering Worksheet": Past Relationship

"IN MY PAST RELATIONSHIP I REALLY DISLIKED…"	
A. List four aspects of your past relationship that complete the sentence *"I really disliked…"*	Now identify from your Personal Fulfillment Needs List the particular need that was missing.
1. Feeling a remoteness when I expressed emotions.	➡ INTIMACY, CONNECTION
2. Not being understood.	➡ INTIMACY, RECOGNITION
3. Being treated as secondary in the relationship.	➡ POWER, RECOGNITION
4. Chasing someone who doesn't share my passion.	➡ ATTENTION, INTIMACY

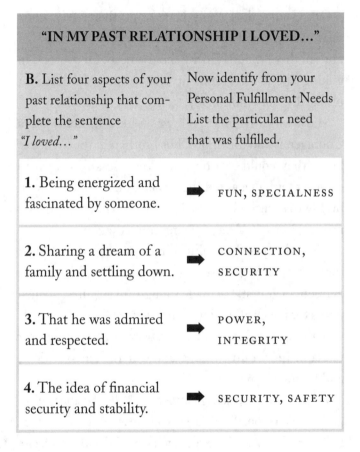

"IN MY PAST RELATIONSHIP I LOVED…"

B. List four aspects of your past relationship that complete the sentence *"I loved…"*

Now identify from your Personal Fulfillment Needs List the particular need that was fulfilled.

1. Being energized and fascinated by someone. ➡ FUN, SPECIALNESS

2. Sharing a dream of a family and settling down. ➡ CONNECTION, SECURITY

3. That he was admired and respected. ➡ POWER, INTEGRITY

4. The idea of financial security and stability. ➡ SECURITY, SAFETY

EXERCISE #4: Worst Relationship

Oh, God… do I really have to go there? My worst relationship stands out like a beacon to all women. Do not sail these waters! Rocky shoals ahead. Of course, I'm talking about a relationship that turned abusive. Not physically, but emotionally.

Mark was a fireman. He was a hero in many ways. Courageous and forthright. His brothers at the firehouse knew they could rely on him. Mark was so driven to service that I always felt there was some terrible event in his life that pushed him to go above and beyond. Always proving himself, always slaying some dragon.

I found myself pursuing him, caught up in a crush that left me not really seeing things straight. Mark was a gentleman at first. He made thoughtful gestures, opened doors for me or offered his arm when walking the streets at night. But as time went on, he began to lose his temper, to blame me for little things, and worst of all, to criticize and humiliate me.

We fell into a repeating pattern of anger and abusive language then reconciling. I eventually reached a point where I thought I had no choice but to stay with Mark. Who else would want me? He made sure my self-esteem was so low that I was grateful for any kindness he showed me.

Those were dark days, and thankfully they didn't last long. With the help of counseling, I realized that his anger and punishing language had nothing to do with me. I decided if he had to work out issues from his past, he could do it without me.

Lucy's "Discovering Worksheet": Worst Relationship

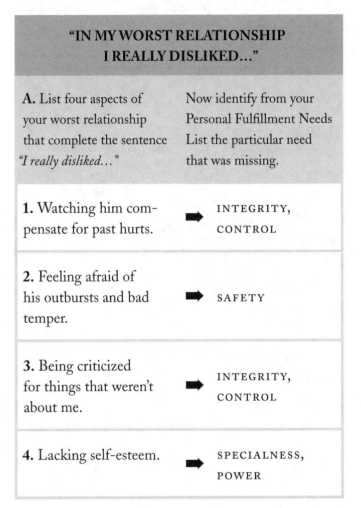

**"IN MY WORST RELATIONSHIP
I REALLY DISLIKED..."**

A. List four aspects of your worst relationship that complete the sentence *"I really disliked..."*

Now identify from your Personal Fulfillment Needs List the particular need that was missing.

1. Watching him compensate for past hurts. ➡ INTEGRITY, CONTROL

2. Feeling afraid of his outbursts and bad temper. ➡ SAFETY

3. Being criticized for things that weren't about me. ➡ INTEGRITY, CONTROL

4. Lacking self-esteem. ➡ SPECIALNESS, POWER

"IN MY WORST RELATIONSHIP I LOVED…"

B. List four aspects of your worst relationship that complete the sentence "*I loved…*"

Now identify from your Personal Fulfillment Needs List the particular need that was fulfilled.

1. Being with someone who was admired and respected. ➡ INTEGRITY

2. Feeling respected and valued at first. ➡ ATTENTION

3. Imagining a life with a secure income. ➡ SECURITY, CONTROL

4. Learning that my self-esteem comes from within. ➡ POWER

CALCULATING THE RESULTS

NOW LUCY'S PERSONAL FULFILLMENT Needs chart is filled in. The Fulfillment Need she identified in each exercise is entered on the next page.

Lucy's Personal Fulfillment Needs List

Need	Exercise #1			Exercise #2			Exercise #3			Exercise #4		
Achievement												
Adventure	✗											
Approval												
Attention	✗						✗			✗		
Community												
Connection	✗						✗	✗				
Control										✗	✗	✗
Fun	✗						✗					
Importance	✗	✗										
Individuality												
➡ Integrity	✗						✗			✗	✗	✗
➡ Intimacy	✗						✗	✗	✗			
Leadership												
➡ Power							✗	✗		✗	✗	
Recognition							✗	✗				
Safety							✗			✗		
➡ Security	✗	✗	✗				✗	✗		✗		
Specialness							✗			✗		

TOP 4 FULFILLMENT NEEDS

INTEGRITY
INTIMACY
POWER
SECURITY

WHAT CHANGED FOR LUCY

YOU KNOW, IF I had just guessed at what my Fulfillment Needs were, rather than follow this process, I think I would have thought fun and adventure would be on the list. And I never would have thought power could be one of my Top 4.

I think I've learned that in order to achieve my actual Top 4, I have to play the long game. Integrity, Intimacy, Power and Security… these needs can form a strong foundation for my life.

I feel wiser now. I can move forward with my life and not rush into things. Maybe my current relationship with Steven will work out, maybe it won't. But now I know the key elements to me having a happy life with someone. I can't wait! Oh, I guess I can.

SELF FULFILLMENT

SOPHIE'S STORY

I'M SOPHIE, AND I'M *sooooo* ready for a change in my life! For the past few years, I've become aware of a growing dissatisfaction with how things have turned out—like I'm somehow missing the point of it all. Surely there's more to life than just working, sleeping, and eating. Don't get me wrong. I love my work as a hairstylist. I get to be creative and to interact with lots of different people (I really enjoy talking to people about their lives), and it pays the bills. No, my job isn't the problem.

My social life is pretty busy. I go out with girlfriends a lot and enjoy dinners, movies, and line dancing at the local country-western bar. My friends are fun and easygoing—we never go too deep into feelings and personal issues—everything's always easy breezy with them. But sometimes (actually, most of the time these days) I feel like I'm standing still, that nothing really changes, and the deeper meanings of my brief time in this world are going unexplored.

It's not that I don't appreciate my friends. I love them! But I'm a happy person when I'm by myself, too. I have a great imagination, which keeps me entertained—I make myself laugh, I'm a scintillating conversationalist (ha-ha!), I like to shake my booty by myself—with the drapes closed, of course. If I could clone myself, I think I'd make a great friend and confidante. Except for my annoying habit of forgetting what I was just talking about and unconsciously eating everything in the fridge... What was I just talking about? Oh yes!

The thing is, I don't think it's really different friends that I need. I just know that there's more to discover about myself and the journey I'm on.

There's a nagging thought I have that quite frankly frightens me sometimes... that I'm missing some key ingredient to my happiness. I think some core need or needs are not being met by this life that I've created. I'm also keenly aware of time passing and don't want to live with the regret that I didn't take action to be my best possible self. I've watched enough Oprah to know there's a more authentic me waiting to be born; I just don't know who that person is yet and what makes her truly happy.

I've been told that this process of identifying my Fulfillment Needs can help me uncover what will bring me the deep satisfaction I'm longing for. I've never been very analytical, but I'm willing to give these exercises a try.

THE UNCOVERING PROCESS

THERE ARE FOUR EXERCISES used to help uncover Fulfillment Needs:

Exercise #1: Narrowing Down the Fulfillment Needs List

Exercise #2: Discovering Worksheet— Current Personal Life Experience

Exercise #3: Discovering Worksheet— Past Personal Life Experience

Exercise #4: Discovering Worksheet— Worst Personal Life Experience

EXERCISE #1: Narrowing Down the List

"Fulfillment"… hmm… I love how that word sounds. It sounds like "fullness" or being "filled up." I already feel like I'm moving in the right direction.

My first task is to review the Master List of Fulfillment Needs and make choices about which needs are important to me and which are less so. I understand that this list represents the majority of needs most people find important and that I can also add my own if I want.

On the next page, you can see the results of my work. I find this process really fun! It makes me realize how diverse people are and that there are lots of ways to be happy. It's just about finding that combination that's unique to me.

Sophie's Narrowed-Down List of Fulfillment Needs	
~~Accomplishment~~	
~~Achievement~~	
~~Acknowledgment~~	
Adventure	Although it wouldn't look like it from the outside, I see myself as an adventurer.
Appreciation	I like to be well thought of.
Approval	I guess this is a hard one to avoid.
Attention	Like from men? Not sure what kind of attention this means.
Autonomy	Maybe.
~~Challenge~~	
~~Community~~	
Connection	I don't know if this a need, but I love people.
Contribution	Yes, for sure.
~~Control~~	
Creativity	I've got so much to offer in this department!
Fairness	Interesting. I'll keep that on the list for now.
Freedom	Yes!
Fun	I think "excitement" might fit better for me.

~~Importance~~	
~~Inclusion~~	
Individuality	That feels right.
Influence	Hmm… not sure, but will keep for now.
Integrity	If that means living up to my own standards.
~~Intimacy~~	
Leadership	In some ways.
Power	I like to see myself as powerful, just not over others.
~~Recognition~~	
~~Safety~~	
~~Security~~	
Specialness	The word feels icky, but I'll get over it.
Uniqueness	I see myself as unique. Maybe it's a need?

EXERCISE #2: Current Personal Life

I define my personal life as the totality of my experiences, but excluding my primary relationship and my job—what I do, feel, and think about when I'm by myself or with friends, and how I view the person I am in relation to the world. I also think my personal life includes my spiritual and philosophical beliefs and the ideas that define my personality.

As I mentioned, I have a fun and gregarious social life. My friends are always looking to have a good time, and I know they appreciate me and enjoy my company. I really like being part of the gang. The problem is they don't really know the real me. I'm afraid if I start to get all serious about topics that are important to me, I'll scare my friends off. But just how much karaoke and line dancing can a person take?!

When I'm by myself, I love reading about spirituality and metaphysical stuff. I like to have my mind blown, to question my assumptions about life, and to discover aspects of my true identity. I know, pretty deep for a hairstylist.

I've started to dabble with meditation, too. My daily life is all chatter, and taking the time to quiet my mind has been really enlightening.

Sophie's "Discovering Worksheet": Current Personal Life

"IN MY CURRENT PERSONAL LIFE I REALLY DISLIKE..."

A. List four aspects of your current personal life that complete the sentence *"I really dislike..."*

Now identify from your Personal Fulfillment Needs List the particular need that is missing.

1. Feeling limited to superficial discussions. ➡ CONNECTION

2. Fear of being viewed as flaky or freaky. ➡ FAIRNESS

3. Worrying my life is being wasted on mundane things. ➡ SPECIALNESS, UNIQUENESS

4. Not exploring new ideas and ways of being. ➡ CREATIVITY

"IN MY CURRENT PERSONAL LIFE I LOVE..."

B. List four aspects of your current personal life that complete the sentence *"I love..."*	Now identify from your Personal Fulfillment Needs List the particular need that is fulfilled.
1. Having a group of friends I can rely on.	➡ CONNECTION
2. Exploring all sorts of concepts about self.	➡ ADVENTURE
3. Making people laugh and feel good.	➡ CONTRIBUTION, FUN
4. Discovering a deep sense of peace and centeredness.	➡ INTEGRITY

EXERCISE #3: Past Personal Life Experience

The happiest times of my life were when I was a child. I loved the endless summers between school years when we'd go up to the cottage and I would spend hours and hours exploring the forests around the lake and day-dreaming in the hammock. My favorite thing was to lie on the boat dock at night and stare up into the stars and try to imagine the unimaginable distances.

I'd hold my hand up outstretched toward the sky and marvel at the silhouette of my fingers superimposed on the Milky Way. How could the universe be so big? How could I be so small? Why am I so small in something so big? Is it all designed just for us? So many questions... so much mystery.

Even as a kid, I knew these questions were important. My parents didn't have the answers... I know, because I asked. They seemed amused by my insatiable curiosity and at the same time appeared a bit uncomfortable that I was so serious about it. I suppose my parents figured Barbies and Easy-Bake ovens should be the high-water mark for self-exploration when you're nine years old. I felt like a bit of an oddity, and that may have started me editing what I said, so my parents would still find me lovable.

My brothers thought I was nuts, so I knew better than to share that part of myself with them. I once hypothesized to them that we couldn't be the only beings in the universe, that other intelligent species must exist—space was just too big! I mean really, have you done the math? Well, for the rest of the summer they called me

"Boobarella," queen of the galaxy. I can laugh now, but I still recall the sting of shame I felt at being labeled and laughed at for just being curious and imaginative. I think my life lesson back then was I needed to be less open with my thoughts and more careful who I shared them with.

Sophie's "Discovering Worksheet": Past Personal Life Experience

"IN MY PAST PERSONAL LIFE I REALLY DISLIKED..."

A. List four aspects of your past personal life experience that complete the sentence *"I really disliked..."*

Now identify from your Personal Fulfillment Needs List the particular need that was missing.

1. Feeling like I couldn't express my curiosity.	➡ FREEDOM, UNIQUENESS
2. Being afraid I was unlovable.	➡ APPROVAL, APPRECIATION
3. Feeling ashamed of being seen as strange.	➡ FREEDOM, APPROVAL
4. Having no one to share my thoughts with.	➡ CONNECTION

"IN MY PAST PERSONAL LIFE I LOVED…"

B. List four aspects of your past personal life experience that complete the sentence *"I loved…"*	Now identify from your Personal Fulfillment Needs List the particular need that was fulfilled.
1. Having time to explore my own imagination.	➡ CREATIVITY, FUN
2. Feeling connected to nature.	➡ ADVENTURE
3. Giving myself permission to reflect deeply.	➡ FREEDOM
4. Developing self-reliance.	➡ POWER

EXERCISE #4: Worst Personal Life Experience

The worst personal life experience for me is beyond a doubt the summer after I graduated from high school. I was so excited to be starting a new life and getting my first job. To really experience freedom for the first time.

But what actually happened was most of my friends moved away, either to go to college or to take jobs away from home. I went from popular and busy in my senior year of high school to adrift, bereft, and disillusioned. It was a rude awakening to the reality that adults have to let go of childhood things and schoolyard friends in order to build a life for themselves. Maybe they covered that in home economics class when I was sick.

I spent months grieving for my old identity. But, as life tends to do, I began to feel stronger and more able. I started making choices for myself, like enrolling in hairdressing school and taking a business course at the community college. I met new friends from all types of backgrounds, and I chose them because I liked them and they shared my interests, not because they lived next door or were on the soccer team.

Sometimes you have to be disassembled a bit in order to become something new and better. That was a hard time of my life, but the bruises were worth it.

Sophie's "Discovering Worksheet": Worst Personal Life Experience

"IN MY WORST PERSONAL LIFE I REALLY DISLIKED…"	
A. List four aspects of your worst personal life experience that complete the sentence *"I really disliked…"*	Now identify from your Personal Fulfillment Needs List the particular need that was missing.
1. Feeling disconnected from my old friends.	➡ CONNECTION
2. Feeling less important in my community.	➡ INFLUENCE, ATTENTION
3. Grieving for an old way of life that was comfortable.	➡ FUN
4. Finding no clear purpose or direction in life.	➡ UNIQUENESS

"IN MY WORST PERSONAL LIFE I LOVED..."

B. List four aspects of your worst personal life experience that complete the sentence *"I loved..."*	Now identify from your Personal Fulfillment Needs List the particular need that was fulfilled.
1. A growing sense of my own power as an adult.	➡ POWER, AUTONOMY
2. Discovering I had choices that were mine to make.	➡ FREEDOM
3. Learning that the world is full of different people.	➡ CONNECTION
4. The feeling of a world of possibilities opening up.	➡ FREEDOM

CALCULATING THE RESULTS

NOW SOPHIE'S PERSONAL FULFILLMENT Needs chart is filled in. The Fulfillment Need she identified in each exercise is entered on the next page.

Sophie's Personal Fulfillment Needs List

	Exercise #1	Exercise #2	Exercise #3	Exercise #4
Adventure	✗		✗	
Appreciation			✗	
Approval			✗ ✗	
Attention				✗
Autonomy				✗
➡ Connection	✗ ✗		✗	✗ ✗
Contribution	✗			
Creativity	✗		✗	
Fairness	✗			
➡ Freedom			✗ ✗ ✗	✗ ✗
➡ Fun	✗		✗	✗
Individuality				
Influence				✗
Integrity	✗			
Leadership				
Power			✗	✗
Specialness	✗			
➡ Uniqueness	✗		✗	✗

TOP 4 FULFILLMENT NEEDS

CONNECTION

FREEDOM

FUN

UNIQUENESS

WHAT CHANGED FOR SOPHIE?

WHAT WAS REALLY SURPRISING for me in completing the exercises by examining different times of my life was that I really do seem to need connection with other people to be really happy and fulfilled. As much as I see myself as the intrepid explorer, I get a lot of joy from being and sharing with others. I can choose to have fun with friends and still be proud of my uniqueness among them.

That doesn't mean that my personal and spiritual journey isn't important. But I see now how I can be creative and find a way to combine these needs into a more fulfilling life that constantly taps into my sources of joy.

I'm so excited to see what I choose next!

NOW IT'S YOUR TURN

The Uncovering Process

THERE ARE FOUR EXERCISES used to help uncover Fulfillment Needs:

> Exercise #1: Narrowing Down the Fulfillment Needs List
>
> Exercise #2: Discovering Worksheet— Current Job, Relationship, or Personal Life Experience
>
> Exercise #3: Discovering Worksheet— Past Job, Relationship, or Personal Life Experience
>
> Exercise #4: Discovering Worksheet— Worst Job, Relationship, or Personal Life Experience

The worksheets in this section use the example of "job" but can be filled in the same way for "relationship" or "personal life," depending on your preference. Keep in mind the following as you fill out your own worksheets:

- Each aspect of your job that you like or don't like may relate to more than one Fulfillment Need. List as many as apply to each aspect.

- You may find that the same need is missing in several aspects of your current job. If so, write it down and put a mark beside that need for each time you identified it as missing.

- The number of marks *(✘)* reveals the importance of a need, whether you've identified it as present or missing.

- After completing all three processes, you may find that some needs on your list have no marks *(✘)* beside them. That tells you they're not among your Top 4.

UNCOVERING YOUR FULFILLMENT NEEDS: YOUR DECISION-MAKING STYLE

PEOPLE MAKE DECISIONS IN different ways. In my book *Law of Connection* I identify the four learning styles people use to make decisions. Knowing and understanding more about your decision-making style will help you work through the processes. Can you recognize and identify your decision-making style?

Some of you may **see** a word and be able to tell right away if it applies to you.

Some of you will find that a word resonates with you; it will **sound** just right for you.

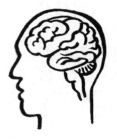

Some of you may **feel** that certain words are right for you. Some may have a gut **feeling** about which words fit and which words don't.

Some of you may have a **knowingness** about which ones should be on your Personal List— they make sense to you.

Exercise #1: Master List of Fulfillment Needs

Accomplishment	
Achievement	
Acknowledgment	
Adventure	
Appreciation	
Approval	
Attention	
Autonomy	
Challenge	
Community	
Connection	
Contribution	
Control	
Creativity	
Fairness	

Freedom	
Fun	
Importance	
Inclusion	
Individuality	
Influence	
Integrity	
Intimacy	
Leadership	
Power	
Recognition	
Safety	
Security	
Specialness	
Uniqueness	

Exercise #2: Discovering Worksheet—Current Job

"IN MY CURRENT JOB I REALLY DISLIKE…"	
A. List four aspects of your current job that complete the sentence *"I really dislike…"*	Now identify from your Personal Fulfillment Needs List the particular need that is missing.
1.	➡
2.	➡
3.	➡
4.	➡

"IN MY CURRENT JOB I LOVE..."

B. List four aspects of your current job that complete the sentence *"I love..."*

Now identify from your Personal Fulfillment Needs List the particular need that is fulfilled.

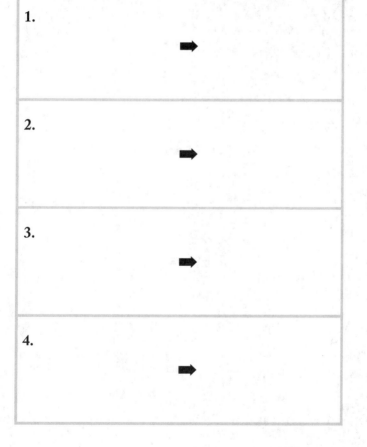

1.

2.

3.

4.

Exercise #3: Discovering Worksheet—Past Job

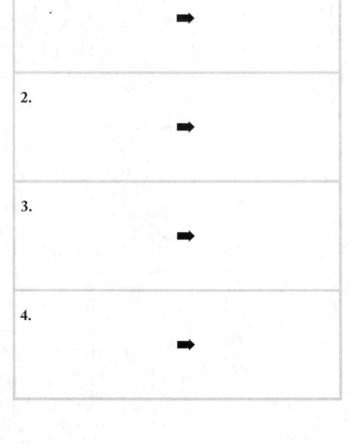

"IN MY PAST JOB I REALLY DISLIKED..."

A. List four aspects of your past job that complete the sentence *"I really disliked..."*

Now identify from your Personal Fulfillment Needs List the particular need that is missing.

1. ➡

2. ➡

3. ➡

4. ➡

"IN MY PAST JOB I LOVED…"

B. List four aspects of your past job that complete the sentence *"I loved…"*

Now identify from your Personal Fulfillment Needs List the particular need that is fulfilled.

1. ➡

2. ➡

3. ➡

4. ➡

Exercise #4: Discovering Worksheet—Worst Job

"IN MY WORST JOB I REALLY DISLIKED..."	
A. List four aspects of your worst job that complete the sentence *"I really disliked..."*	Now identify from your Personal Fulfillment Needs List the particular need that is missing.
1. ➡	
2. ➡	
3. ➡	
4. ➡	

"IN MY WORST JOB I LOVED..."

B. List four aspects of your worst job that complete the sentence *"I loved..."*

Now identify from your Personal Fulfillment Needs List the particular need that is fulfilled.

1. ➡

2. ➡

3. ➡

4. ➡

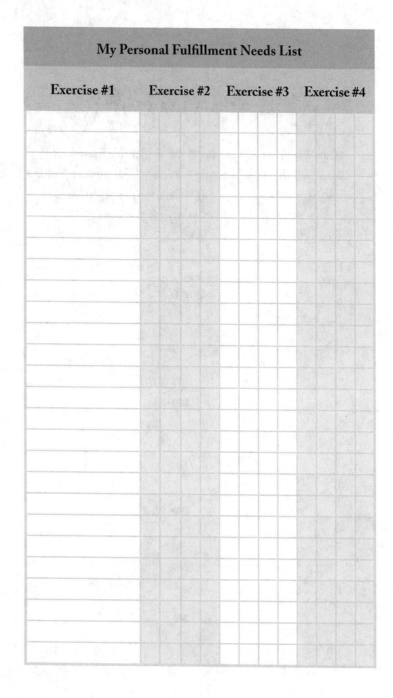

APPLYING

NOW THAT I KNOW, WHAT DO I DO?

NOT KNOWING WHAT FULFILLS you can often lead to getting involved with people, situations, and jobs that don't feel good. Hopefully, you now understand that the reason something doesn't feel good is that it is not meeting your needs. That's why it's so important to know what your Fulfillment Needs are.

Now that you know your Top 4 Fulfillment Needs, you can start using that information as a yardstick or measuring tool to help you make decisions.

One of my top Fulfillment Needs is to influence people in a positive way. So it brings me lots of satisfaction when I hear from people who have gone through the processes and are excited to tell me what they're now doing differently.

Here are a few examples of how people are using their newfound self-awareness to improve their lives.

Many report that they're using their Top 4 when doing a job search to determine what will satisfy and fulfill them. Some are reporting that their Top 4 Fulfillment Needs are even more of a deciding factor than the salary.

Others are reporting that their rapport with their business partners and coworkers has improved since they've learned about one another's Fulfillment Needs. Some business teams report feeling more connected to one another now that the whole team has worked through the processes and are considering one another's needs. Some teams have even created a report that lists all the team members' Fulfillment Needs!

Others say that they are using this information to improve their existing relationships. Now that they're aware of each other's Fulfillment Needs, they are making a conscious effort to help get them met, or at least be mindful of them.

HOW I APPLIED KNOWING MY FULFILLMENT NEEDS TO MY BUSINESS

SINCE I UNCOVERED MY Top 4 Fulfillment Needs, I have created a life and business that allow me to get my Fulfillment Needs met on a daily basis. All of my decisions are determined by whether I will get one or more of my Fulfillment Needs met.

Check out my strategies, keeping in mind my Top 4 Fulfillment Needs, attention, positive influence, intimacy, and freedom.

MY STRATEGIES FOR GETTING
MY FULFILLMENT NEEDS MET

☐ Full-day seminars (1-2 times a month)

☐ Presentations (1-2 times a month)

☐ Book signings

☐ Radio interviews (2-3 times a week)

☐ Facebook page

☐ Teleclasses with students

☐ Coaching and mentoring

"Hey, Michael,
I hear there's a job opening
for a crane operator.
It will double your salary.
Are you interested?"

"Hmm, let's see...
Would I get any of my Top 4
Fulfillment Needs met?"

NOW IT'S YOUR TURN

CAN YOU IMAGINE WAYS to incorporate what you've learned about your own Top 4 to improve your life? Take some time to explore and consider the observations and insights that are surely becoming clearer as you continue to make connections between past experiences and your newly uncovered Fulfillment Needs.

Will you make a commitment to yourself to do more of the things that meet your needs? You'll now have heightened awareness of when you're doing something that doesn't fulfill you. If you have to do things that don't fulfill you, try to get through them quickly!

What strategies can you build into *your* life so that your Top 4 needs are met on a regular basis?

MY STRATEGIES FOR GETTING
MY FULFILLMENT NEEDS MET

THIS SECTION SUMMARY AND CHECKLIST

IN THIS SECTION WE discovered:

- ☐ That we can use our top Fulfillment Needs to help us make decisions

- ☐ That we can create strategies that help us get our Fulfillment Needs met on a regular basis

GETTING MORE CLARITY ON YOUR TOP 4

ARE YOU USING POSITIVE OR NEGATIVE WAYS TO GET YOUR FULFILLMENT NEEDS MET?

NOW THAT YOU'VE IDENTIFIED your Top 4 (or more) Fulfillment Needs, here's an exercise to test the accuracy of your chosen Top 4 and perhaps reveal which one is the strongest and most important to you.

Perhaps you had the same number of marks for several Fulfillment Needs and can't decide which ones are strongest. Or maybe you have one Fulfillment Need that had many marks, but you're still not sure if it fits.

One way to test which Fulfillment Needs should be in your Top 4 (or identify which need is strongest) is to ask yourself this question: Was there a time in the past when I used a negative or ineffective strategy for getting this Fulfillment Need met?

In most cases, if it's one of your top Fulfillment Needs, the answer will be yes.

For example, to help you decide if Attention is one of your top Fulfillment Needs, ask yourself if you've ever used negative ways to get that need for attention met. In other words, were you the class clown? Were you the show-off? Answering yes may be a good indication that Attention is one of your top Fulfillment Needs.

Or how about Approval? Did you ever use negative ways to get someone's approval? If you can recall a time when you would do absolutely anything to get attention or approval, you know you're on the right track in choosing them for your Top 4.

POSITIVE AND NEGATIVE STRATEGIES

POSITIVE AND NEGATIVE STRATEGIES FOR MEETING FULFILLMENT NEEDS		
Flo's Fulfillment Needs	Met Through a Positive Strategy	Met Through a Negative Strategy
Connection	Being sociable at work	Trying too hard to be liked
Freedom	Giving myself one free day a week to do as I please	Canceling commitments with family and friends
Fun	Organizing events and dinner parties	In my younger years, I sometimes made fun of people

Now it's your turn. List your Top 4 Fulfillment Needs in the following chart and try to recall times when you used positive and negative ways to get them met. Add rows underneath if you have more than four to reflect on.

POSITIVE AND NEGATIVE STRATEGIES FOR MEETING FULFILLMENT NEEDS		
Your Fulfillment Needs	Met Through a Positive Strategy	Met Through a Negative Strategy

You may notice that you used more negative strategies to get one of your Top 4 Fulfillment Needs met than you did for any of the others. Pay attention to that; it may mean that this one is your most dominant need.

152

THE STICKY NOTE PROCESS: HOW TO PUT YOUR TOP 4 IN ORDER

Ideally, by the end of this exercise, you'll have arranged your Top 4 Fulfillment Needs in order of importance.

1: Use Your Intuition

Write one of your top Fulfillment Needs on each of four (or more) sticky notes. Think about each one. Does it fit? Does it make sense? Does it sound like you? Do you see yourself that way?

As you think about each need, use your intuition to put them in order from first and strongest to least important. Post the sticky notes on a wall or a bulletin board arranged so that the most important need is on top and the weakest is on the bottom, as shown on the next page. Keep moving the notes around until you find the order that feels right, the one that makes the most sense to you, the one that looks correct.

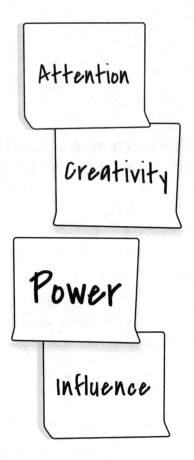

2: Recall Unhappy or Unfulfilling Events

Recall and observe past events and times when you *weren't* fulfilled. Memorable events that made you unhappy are a good indication that your needs were not getting met. Whenever you recall an event you didn't like, go to your sticky notes and try to identify which of your needs were not being fulfilled.

This exercise can be a powerful way to uncover the Fulfillment Needs that are most important to you.

It's often easier to remember events or occasions when you weren't experiencing joy, and now that you've uncovered your Top 4 Fulfillment Needs and begun to put them in order, you can start to understand why you were so unhappy.

For example, Joe, who is one of my clients, determined that Acknowledgment was one of his Top 4. He had a strong memory of a time when he'd worked nights and weekends to complete a special project for his boss and didn't get any acknowledgment for his effort. He remembers feeling angry and resentful, and now he realizes it was because his need for Acknowledgment is so strong.

3: Recall Happy or Fulfilling Events

Recall and observe experiences that *have* brought you joy. Any time you find yourself saying, "Wow! I really loved it when *that* happened," consider which of your Fulfillment Needs were being met. This may give you a new understanding of *why* you felt so good.

Joe was also able to clearly recall a time when he helped his elderly neighbors prune a tree in their yard. For years afterward they acknowledged his help by mentioning it every time they waved to him over the fence or hosted a neighborhood potluck. Now he understands why this meant so much to him.

4: Think of a Time You Made a Major Decision

- Left a relationship or ended a friendship
- Embraced a relationship or started a new friendship
- Left a job
- Accepted a job
- Bought a major appliance or home
- Chose one vacation over another
- Bought a specific home or vehicle
- Left a volunteer position
- Took a new volunteer position
- Joined a group or a club
- Left a group or a club

What was it that helped you make those decisions? Does it make more sense now? Do you better understand why you added something to your life, or why you removed it from your life?

Do you see and understand the relationship between the decisions you made and what your Fulfillment Needs are?

5: Notice What's Making You Feel Fulfilled Right Now

As soon as you have an experience of being totally fulfilled, go to your sticky notes and look at the order. Notice which Fulfillment Needs were met in that experience, and which one was most important. Move your sticky notes around to change the order, if necessary. The next fulfilling experience you have, notice again which needs were met and if the order still feels right.

Get in the habit of referring back to your Fulfillment Needs list until you can recall them easily and use them to assess any situation.

Eventually you may notice that many of your past experiences connect to one need in particular. That could be a good indication that this Fulfillment Need is very important to you. Pay attention, acknowledge it's important to you, and consider moving that sticky note to the top position of your list.

You might rearrange your sticky notes several times before the order feels right to you. Go back to them on a regular basis and keep checking your word order until you are satisfied. The purpose of the sticky notes is to train you to keep looking at your Top 4 Fulfillment Needs and really see their importance to you.

There may have been a time when you thought *all thirty* of the Fulfillment Needs applied to you, but now you've narrowed them down to your Top 4.

Way to go! You've come a long way. Congratulations!

THIS SECTION SUMMARY AND CHECKLIST

IN THIS SECTION WE discovered:

☐ That we can use positive and negative strategies for getting our Fulfillment Needs met

☐ How to reflect on our experiences and use this information to help put our top Fulfillment Needs in order of importance

☐ That we can use the suggestions provided to put our top Fulfillment Needs in order

☐ That we can keep changing the order until it feels right and makes sense to us

HOW KNOWING ABOUT FULFILLMENT NEEDS WILL IMPACT YOUR RELATIONSHIPS

FULFILLMENT IN RELATIONSHIPS

NOW THAT YOU UNDERSTAND your own Fulfillment Needs, you can share these processes and support others in identifying and meeting their needs, which will significantly improve your relationships with them.

In some cases, even if you can't share the processes, you may be able to observe others, guess what their Fulfillment Needs might be, and improve your relationship and communication on your own. You may be surprised by the impact your new awareness can have.

WHAT OTHERS ARE SAYING

"KNOWING YOUR FULFILLMENT NEEDS is like a short-cut to happiness with your partner. It eliminates the guessing games and power struggles and allows for each person to be who they really are! There is a mutual understanding and compassion that bonds you together. The day-to-day of the relationship is much more fun, and when life hands you challenges, you face them as a solid team."
—Michelle Berting Brett

"When my husband and I uncovered our Fulfillment Needs, we got much-needed clarity on where we each were coming from. Suddenly, arriving at big and little decisions became much easier, because we understood the fundamental motivations that bring joy into our lives, individually and as a couple. It is our opinion that uncovering our Fulfillment Needs provided us with an essential tool to understand

each other's perspectives a lot faster and much easier than many, many sessions of marital counseling could ever do. Like with Law of Attraction, *Michael has done it again—he has provided us with a wonderful how-to guide."* —Adriana Gendron

YOUR PRIMARY RELATIONSHIP

HAVE YOU NOTICED SOMEONE (perhaps you?) complaining about not feeling fulfilled in their primary relationship?

It's also likely that you know people who *are* fulfilled in their primary relationship; you can tell just by being around them.

When you went through the Uncovering Process looking at your primary relationship, you probably uncovered why and where some of your needs were not being met in your current and past relationships.

When you and your partner know and support each other's Fulfillment Needs, you can improve the harmony and communication between you.

How do you get started? Ideally, both you and your partner are interested in learning how to increase the fulfillment you experience with each other and within yourselves.

My clients Brenda and Paul had been married eight years and had a young family. They both wanted to feel more fulfilled in their relationship. I first led each of them through the processes to uncover their Top 4 Fulfillment Needs:

Brenda's Fulfillment Needs: Autonomy, Control, Safety, and Contribution

Paul's Fulfillment Needs: Attention, Leadership, Influence, and Contribution

After that I asked them to share what they'd uncovered about their needs with each other. In addition to gaining a greater understanding of their own Fulfillment Needs, each of them now had a new awareness of the other's needs. They each realized that in the past they hadn't given a lot of thought to what might fulfill the other.

BRENDA'S RELATIONSHIP WORKSHEET

After completing the processes to uncover your Top 4 Fulfillment Needs and sharing them with your partner, answer the following questions.

(1) What did you learn about yourself?

In the past, I felt embarrassed to want to have Autonomy (or to like being on my own sometimes). Now I understand it is important to me; it's fulfilling. And when things are in my Control, that makes me feel good, too. Overall, I like being able to identify what Fulfillment Need is making me feel good.

MICHAEL J. LOSIER

(2) What did you learn about your partner?

I didn't realize that Attention was so important
to Paul, and that my need for Autonomy sometimes conflicted with that. I also learned that one
of the ways he Contributes is through providing
Leadership.

**(3) What will you do differently in your relation-
ship now?**

Now that I know our Fulfillment Needs, I can take
ownership of getting my needs met and support
Paul to do the same. I can try letting him "lead,"
plan more of our trips, and find ways to give him
the attention he needs.

**(4) What suggestions can you give your partner to
support him/her in helping you fulfill your Top 4
needs?**

My Needs	My Suggestions for Paul
1. *Autonomy*	We could designate a room in the house where I can be alone and do my thing. It would help me to feel okay to do that if I knew I had Paul's support.
2. *Control*	Because Control is important to me, it would help if Paul could remember my need to stay on track with my plans. He tends to get excited with new ideas, and it would help if he could find ways to pursue them that didn't upset my plans.
3. *Safety*	I am in the process of transitioning into my own business, so knowing he would be there for me (financially) would make me feel safe.
4. *Contribution*	We both like to contribute. We have been doing this together for years. It's our happiest time together. We will do more of it more often.

RELATIONSHIP WORKSHEET

Now it's your turn.

After completing the processes to uncover your Top 4 Fulfillment Needs and sharing them with your partner, answer the following questions.

(1) What did you learn about yourself?

_____

_____

_____

_____

_____

_____

_____

(2) What did you learn about your partner?

_____
_____
_____
_____
_____
_____
_____

(3) What will you do differently in your relationship now?

_____
_____
_____
_____
_____

(4) What suggestions can you give your partner to support him/her in helping to fulfill your Top 4 needs?

Fill in answers on next page.

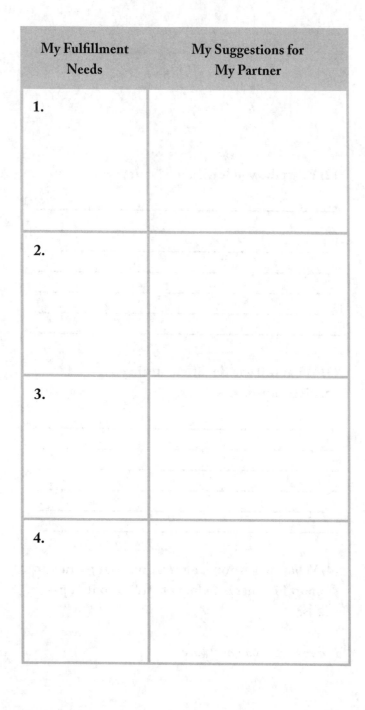

My Fulfillment Needs	My Suggestions for My Partner
1.	
2.	
3.	
4.	

Post both your Fulfillment Needs in a place where you can be reminded of them regularly. Continue to reflect on your primary relationship and try to find creative ways to support each other in getting your Fulfillment Needs met.

APPLYING FULFILLMENT NEEDS
TO OTHER RELATIONSHIPS

BRENDA AND PAUL ALSO used their knowledge of Fulfillment Needs to improve their communication and relationships with their daughters, age six and seven. They had been observing the children and had a good idea of what their Fulfillment Needs were. That knowledge makes a huge difference in how they connect and communicate with their children.

Here is what Brenda and Paul believed were their older daughter's top Fulfillment Needs.

Older Child's Fulfillment Needs	As parents, now that we know...
1. Attention	We have taught our daughter that she can get our attention and have our attentiveness when she needs it.
2. Acknowledgment	We can do a better job of acknowledging her more often—especially by using the word "acknowledge" in our communication.

Here is what Brenda and Paul believed were their younger daughter's top Fulfillment Needs.

Younger Child's Fulfillment Needs	As parents, now that we know...
1. Autonomy	We can respect our daughter's request to be alone to read a book or play by herself.
2. Control	We can give her tasks that she is in charge of, such as a weekly chore or monthly responsibility.

APPLYING FULFILLMENT NEEDS
TO YOUR BUSINESS TEAM

WHEN THREE BUSINESS PARTNERS who were running an Internet company brought me in to help with their communication problems, I quickly observed that one of the partners sometimes repeated himself in an effort to be heard and acknowledged.

I guessed that Acknowledgment might be one of his top Fulfillment Needs and asked what it was like for him to present an idea to his partners. He told me he often felt frustrated when they merely nodded or sometimes did not reply at all to his e-mails. When he didn't feel heard or acknowledged, it was difficult for him to brainstorm with the others.

His partners were surprised to hear that he wasn't feeling acknowledged and didn't realize how important that was to him. Because it wasn't a strong need for them, they hadn't been aware that he needed it. Once they found out, they agreed to make a conscious effort to acknowledge his contributions.

We discussed their mutual goal, which was to have a healthy, harmonious, prosperous business, and how knowing and working with one another's Fulfillment Needs could help them achieve that.

THIS SECTION SUMMARY AND CHECKLIST

IN THIS SECTION WE discovered:

- ☐ Knowing my partner's and my top Fulfillment Needs can greatly enhance our relationship and communication

- ☐ We can find ways to support each other in getting our top Fulfillment Needs met

- ☐ Other types of relationships can also be enhanced by knowing and supporting our Fulfillment Needs

USING THE LAW OF ATTRACTION TO SATISFY YOUR FULFILLMENT NEEDS

APPLYING THE LAW OF ATTRACTION TO ATTRACT FULFILLING OPPORTUNITIES

NOW THAT YOU HAVE a better understanding of what fulfills you, it's time to tap into the Law of Attraction to deliberately attract the opportunities, ideas, and information that will help you satisfy your Fulfillment Needs.

In my first book, *Law of Attraction*, I explained how we could attract more of what we want and less of what we don't want into our lives. The words we use and the thoughts we think cause us to send out a vibe (vibration), and what we attract matches the vibrations we put out. Life is energy, and energy attracts like energy.

In simplest terms, the Law of Attraction means that we attract into our lives whatever we give our attention, energy, and focus to, whether positive or negative.

WORDS AND THOUGHTS
CREATE VIBES

Words	Thoughts	Vibes +/-

I HAVE MANY EXAMPLES in own my life of attracting opportunities that satisfy all of my top Fulfillment Needs. You can, too!

Law of Attraction Step 1:

Identify what you want. In this book, you've already done that by identifying your Fulfillment Needs and some strategies for getting them met.

Law of Attraction Step 2:

Give attention, energy, and focus to your desire, so that you are sending out a positive vibration for the Law of Attraction to match.

To help you with Step 2, here are three sample scripts you can use to help you give attention, energy, and focus to the needs you desire to fulfill. The scripts are deliberately designed to give positive attention to your desires.

How to Give Attention to Your Desires

SCRIPT 1: "I'm in the process of attracting and allowing everything I need to do, know, and have in order to bring in opportunities to fulfill my Top 4 needs of _____, _____, _____, and _____ (fill in the blanks). I love knowing that the Law of Attraction is unfolding and orchestrating whatever has to happen in order for me to live a rich, fulfilled life of joy through positive strategies for getting my needs met."

SCRIPT 2: "I love the thought of attracting resources and information that will lead me to the strategies I need to get my Fulfillment Needs met. I love knowing that the Law of Attraction will bring to me contacts, information, and resources that are in alignment with getting my Top 4 Fulfillment Needs met."

SCRIPT 3: "I love knowing that the Law of Attraction is unfolding and orchestrating whatever needs to happen to bring to me what I need to attract, so I can live a life of joy through fulfilling my needs. I love attracting strategies that I can apply to fulfill my needs in positive ways."

Feel free to adjust these scripts to fit your needs and desires. Try inserting your Top 4 Fulfillment Needs into the scripts, or create your own scripts that incorporate your needs and feel good as you say them. Post them where you can read them often.

Remember: the more you give attention, energy, and focus to your desires, the stronger and clearer the vibration you are sending for the Law of Attraction to match.

Law of Attraction Step 3:

Remove doubt so that you allow things to come to you. You can do that by noticing and acknowledging (celebrating) the things showing up in your life that are in alignment with getting your Fulfillment Needs met.

Tell yourself things like, "I notice that I'm attracting information, people, and resources that are in alignment with having my Fulfillment Needs met."

As you're using the Law of Attraction to attract strategies to meet your Fulfillment Needs, you may find you are attracting only pieces of a strategy or idea. In other words, the whole strategy might not come to you right away. Notice the things that *are* coming. Keep track of the number of things you are attracting that are in alignment with your Fulfillment Needs. This will help you to believe that it *is* possible for you to attract what you need.

You'll be sending out positive vibes when you keep track of the number of positive things you are attracting.

THIS SECTION SUMMARY AND CHECKLIST

IN THIS SECTION WE discovered:

☐ We can use the Law of Attraction deliberately to attract opportunities, ideas, and information to help us get our Fulfillment Needs met

☐ The more we give attention, energy, and focus to our desires, the more we are sending out a clear vibration for the Law of Attraction to match

☐ It's important to notice and acknowledge things that *are* showing up in our lives that are in alignment with getting our Fulfillment Needs met

DAILY PRACTICE SEVEN-DAY
OBSERVATION LOG

DAILY PRACTICE IN
SATISFYING YOUR TOP 4

NOW THAT YOU UNDERSTAND more about satisfying
your Top 4 Fulfillment Needs, it's time to make sure that
you have a greater understanding of how this knowledge
will impact all areas of your life.

To do that, you'll need to spend some more time
consciously observing patterns. When you are feeling
great, observe what need is being met in that moment,
in order to make sure you're meeting your Top 4 in a
constructive way.

The following Seven-Day Observation Log is designed
to help you stay connected to this process. You'll make
many observations and have "aha moments" as you start
to notice the difference in your level of happiness when
you're getting your Fulfillment Needs met as opposed
to when you're not, and you'll quickly learn to make all

of your decisions based on getting your Fulfillment Needs met.

This is a self-exploratory process, an opportunity to integrate your understanding and learn more about how to get your Fulfillment Needs met. Keep this log in a place where you can easily record your observations and insights.

FULFILLMENT NEEDS
SEVEN-DAY OBSERVATION LOG

Date: _____   Day #_____

What I'm noticing and doing differently now that I am aware of my Fulfillment Needs.

In my primary relationships

_____

_____

_____

_____

_____

_____

_____

_____

In my work/career

_____

_____

_____

_____

_____

_____

_____

In my friendships

_____

_____

_____

_____

_____

_____

_____

In my general life

_____

_____

_____

_____

_____

_____

_____

(Download this log at www.YourLifesPurposeBook.com)

⊙

INTERPRETIVE GLOSSARY OF
FULFILLMENT NEEDS

THIS GLOSSARY OF FULFILLMENT Needs may help to clarify the meanings of the words.

It is called an interpretive glossary because I've used the interpretations and definitions of many people in order to create it.

Remember, you can reframe the meanings to fit your own interpretation of the words. You can even combine words if that feels right and makes sense to you.

It's your interpretation that matters!

Accomplishment

- Something that has been attained successfully (e.g., the reduction of his personal debt was a remarkable accomplishment).

- The successful completion of a task (e.g., finishing her degree was quite an accomplishment).

Achievement

- Something done successfully, typically by effort, courage, or skill (e.g., they felt justifiably proud of their achievement).

- To attain a desired level of performance (e.g., her achievement in her sport is remarkable), usually acknowledged through rewards, awards, or certificates.

Acknowledgment

- An expression (often verbal) of recognition or appreciation for something someone has done (e.g., Mary's husband's compliments were just the acknowledgment she'd been hoping for).

- The act of showing that one has noticed someone or something (e.g., he felt fulfilled by the acknowledgment when his donation was mentioned in the newsletter).

Adventure

- An exciting activity, often spontaneous, typically hazardous, especially the daring exploration of unknown territory and/or the pursuit of novel experiences (e.g., she traveled the world in search of adventure).

- Incurring risk of some kind (e.g., he was adventurous even in his choice of investments).

Appreciation

- The recognition and enjoyment of the good qualities in someone or something: (e.g., I smiled in appreciation of her helpful gesture).

- Gratitude for someone's contribution or action (e.g., she expressed her appreciation for his hard work).

Approval

- The belief that someone or something is good or acceptable (e.g., actors need to win the audience's approval).

- The expression of a favorable opinion (e.g., she hoped for her mother's approval of her outfit).

Attention

- Notice taken of someone or something; the regarding of someone or something as interesting or important (e.g., she loved the attention she got for her original dance moves).

- Giving special care and consideration to a task (e.g., he gave the problem his full attention).

Autonomy

- Freedom from external control or influence; personal independence (e.g., she loved the autonomy of being her own boss).

- You can do it alone. You can do it on your own. You like it best that way (e.g., he didn't need to be on a team to get a project done, and he performed better when he wasn't micromanaged).

Challenge

- A task or situation that tests someone's abilities (e.g., the steep mountain is a challenge for experienced climbers).

- An opportunity to prove or stretch oneself (e.g., he loved to challenge himself by playing against more experienced chess players).

Community

- A feeling of fellowship with others as a result of sharing common attitudes, interests, and goals (e.g., she longed for the sense of community that belonging to her church provided).

- Feeling a bond with a group of people (e.g., he loved the sense of community at the local farmers' market).

Connection

- Feeling joined or united with someone (e.g., she loved the feeling of connection when they held hands during their walks).

- People with whom one has social or professional contact or to whom one is related, especially those with influence who are able to offer one help (e.g., he had connections to important businessmen who were able to help him make decisions).

Contribution

- The part played by a person or thing in bringing about a result or helping something to advance (e.g., her donation to the shelter was a valuable contribution).

- The act of giving toward a common purpose (e.g., his contribution of supplies allowed the boys to continue with their project).

Control

- The power to influence or direct people's behavior or the course of events (e.g., the whole operation is under the control of a production manager).

- Managing the arrangement or position of people or things in relation to one another in accordance with a particular sequence, or method; this includes ensuring adherence to a prescribed or established procedure (e.g., in his new position, he had more control over customer follow-up procedures).

Creativity

- Showing original thought; the quality of being inventive, inspiring, ingenious (e.g., she brought a fresh creativity to her problem-solving sessions).

- Use of the imagination or original ideas, often in artistic endeavors (e.g., his designs showed a level of creativity that impressed his supervisor).

Fairness

- Being just or appropriate in the circumstances (e.g., her curfew was fair, given the poor judgment she had shown); or being treated fairly.

- Doing something without cheating or trying to achieve unjust advantage (e.g., he always made sure the game was played fairly).

Freedom

- The power or right to act, speak, or think as one wants without hindrance or restraint (e.g., he loved having the freedom to change his routine every so often).

- The state of being physically unrestricted and able to move easily (e.g., the freedom to move to a warmer climate was something she'd looked forward to).

Fun

- Enjoyment, amusement, or lighthearted pleasure; playful behavior or good humor (e.g., she realized she was missing some fun in her life).

- A behavior or activity that is intended purely for amusement (e.g., he'd forgotten how much fun he had playing the guitar).

Importance

- Of great significance or value; likely to have a profound effect on success, survival, or well-being (e.g., he liked knowing that he was an important contributor to the project).

- Having high rank, status, dignity, or authority (e.g., she was a woman of great importance).

Inclusion

- Being regarded as belonging to a larger group or structure (e.g., when he made the team, he felt a sense of inclusion for the first time).

- Being involved in planning or decision making (e.g., she loved being old enough to be included in the family holiday planning).

Individuality

- The qualities or character that distinguish one person from others who are similar, especially when strongly marked (e.g., her choice in clothes showed real style and individuality).

- To be separate, distinct, or independent of others, to not conform to the majority (e.g., his parents taught him to value his sense of individuality, even when he didn't always fit in).

Influence

- The capacity to have an effect on the character, development, or behavior of someone or something (e.g., as a mentor, he was a good influence on the students).

- The ability to persuade others toward an outcome (e.g., she was able to influence her fellow staff members to vote for a job-sharing option).

Integrity

- The quality of being honest and having strong moral principles; moral uprightness (e.g., he is known to be a man of integrity).

- Doing what you say you're going to do; saying yes when you mean yes, and saying no when you mean no (e.g., she valued integrity in her commitments).

Intimacy

- Close familiarity or friendship; social closeness, especially between two people, that is conducive to the exchange of ideas and personal information (e.g., the couple's level of intimacy increased after the workshop).

- A private, cozy atmosphere (e.g., she redecorated the bedroom to create a feeling of intimacy).

Leadership

- The act of leading a group of people or an organization (e.g., the members looked to her for leadership during the transition).

- Offering guidance and direction to others (e.g., finding himself in a leadership role on the project boosted his confidence).

Power

- The capacity or ability to direct or influence the behavior of others or the course of events (e.g., he had the power to determine the length of the proceedings).

- Having a personal sense of control over one's own life (e.g., she finally felt like she had the power to decide how she wanted to live her life).

Recognition

- Appreciation or acclaim for an achievement, service, or ability (e.g., she received the award in recognition of her courageous human rights work).

- Acknowledgment for one's actions or position (e.g., he loved the recognition that came from touring with the band).

Safety

- The condition of being protected from injury (e.g., he felt safer with the climbing harness on).

- Freedom from danger or risks (e.g., she felt safety in traveling with a group rather than on her own).

Security

- The state of feeling free from fear, worry, or anxiety (e.g., his new job and salary gave him an increased sense of security).

- A feeling of assurance and protection (e.g., she liked the level of security she felt in her new apartment building).

Specialness

- Better, greater, or otherwise different from what is usual; exceptionally good or precious (e.g., she loved how special his thoughtfulness made her feel).

- Known for a particular quality or task (e.g., he was often chosen for special assignments due to his specific skill set).

Uniqueness

- Being the only one; unlike anyone else (e.g., her designs made her unique in her field).

- Being one of a kind, an original (e.g., each of her designs was unique; there were no two alike).

AFTERWORD

MY HUNCH IS THAT things have changed for you since you've uncovered your Top 4 Fulfillment Needs. Some of you may have already changed jobs, clients, or relationships because you were not getting your needs met. Some of you are thinking about how to make some changes— that is, how to be more deliberate about getting your Fulfillment Needs met.

This information is probably new to you. Be gentle with yourself as you uncover the areas in your life that are not fulfilling and develop the courage to make changes based on what *would* fulfill you and bring you more joy.

Imagine how it would feel to surround yourself with others who are also fulfilled in their lives. How can you do that? By introducing this book and its processes to your family, friends, work teams, and others with whom you have relationships.

Care enough about yourself and others to support one another in experiencing more joy.

Say YES to getting your Fulfillment Needs met!

Take care,

—Michael

ABOUT THE AUTHOR

Michael Losier (Low-zee-eh) lives in beautiful Victoria, British Columbia, on Canada's West Coast. He is the author of the best-selling books *Law of Attraction: The Science of Attracting More of What You Want and Less of What You Don't* and *Law of Connection: The Science of Using NLP to Create Ideal Personal and Professional Relationships*.

To satisfy the many people wanting to learn how to apply the Law of Attraction, Michael developed a Certified Law of Attraction Facilitator program and has trained and certified more than 320 people in fourteen countries to teach others the Law of Attraction. Training others is one of the ways Michael gets his Fulfillment Needs met!

Michael is so passionate about teaching that he travels the world sharing his insight into the Law of Attraction, delivering hundreds of hours of teleclasses, podcasts, workshops, and seminars every year. His YouTube videos have millions of views.

Michael was interviewed by Oprah Winfrey four times for her Soul Series on Oprah Radio™ on SiriusXM satellite radio. He also enjoyed a yearlong run as the weekly Law of Attraction radio host on Oprah Radio™.

Michael is an avid hiker, enjoying Canada's West Coast, which boasts some of the most beautiful coastal and old-growth forested trails in the country.

Here's how to stay connected with Michael:

www.HangOutWithMichael.com

www.YourLifesPurposeBook.com

Facebook.com/MichaelLosierFans

Worksheets are available at www.YourLifesPurposeBook.com